⭐⭐⭐⭐⭐ REVIEWPERSTAR ⭐⭐⭐⭐⭐
12 Tasteful Ways to Get More Book Reviews

By Buck Flogging

http://www.archangelink.com

March 2014
Copyright © 2014 Archangel Ink
All rights reserved worldwide.

♦ Published by Archangel Ink

ISBN 149741511X
ISBN-13: 978-1497415119

Disclaimer

I will not be held accountable for the success or failure of any changes to your online business model that reading this book inspires. Each writer, website, subject matter, and business model has its own subtle uniqueness that must be taken into consideration when making any decision. What works in one niche and for one person can be an abysmal failure for another person in a different niche. Please think carefully about your own audience and factors that are unique to your business when considering making any changes.

I will also not be held accountable for any breaches of Amazon's review policies (http://amzn.to/1jbJ6Li) or actions taken against you by Amazon or other vendors. These policies are always changing, and you should refer to them before attempting any of the review strategies outlined in this book.

Table of Contents

My Reviewsumé   6

Becoming a Reviewperstar   10

Review Strategy1: Build a Following   14

Review Strategy 2: Write a Good Book   19

Review Strategy 3: Keep It Short   26

Review Strategy 4: Call for Review   29

Review Strategy 5: KDP Select   33

Review Strategy 6: TwiggleFace+ Tricks   38

Review Strategy 7: Email Signature   42

Review Strategy 8: Write Reviews   45

Review Strategy 9: Audible Discount Codes   48

B.D.P. Strategies

Review Strategy 10: Build a Review Team   51

Review Strategy 11: Gift Card Idea   71

Review Strategy 12: Build a Network   83

Conclusion   87

Other Recommended Author Resources   90

Excerpt from *How to Create an Audiobook for Audible*   91

About the Author   103

My Reviewsumé

Hi, I'm Buck Flogging. As shocking as it may sound, that's not my real name. So if you are looking on Buck's author page for signs of review-bagging mastery, you're looking in the wrong place. This book clearly will get a lot of reviews though, because I know you wouldn't dare to NOT leave a review for this thing when you're done. That would be criminal.

Seriously, if this thing only gets like seven reviews, that's going to be pretty embarrassing. Please don't embarrass Buck. He's very fragile for a guy who can squat 800 pounds and bring four women to simultaneous orgasm with his hands tied behind his back.

Full disclosure, as I write this very sentence I've gotten around 900 reviews from all of my books combined, not including the few dozen on some of the books I pulled down for revision back in November of 2013. By the time you read this, I'll probably have over a thousand. I got an amazing 600 reviews in the three months prior to writing this book from implementing many of the strategies outlined in this lil' fella.

Much of this is attributable, not to huge volumes of book sales, but to a variety of simple strategies that I have executed to perfection. Some of it *is* attributable to sizeable volumes of downloads through Amazon's KDP Select program, which enables authors to get huge volumes of free downloads if they play their cards right. Free promotions have been bashed a lot lately and called "dead," but there are still compelling reasons to take advantage of this strategy if you know how to properly leverage it to your advantage. One of those reasons is getting more reviews, which have a significant impact on your book's long-term salability and your overall image as a writer.

It's certainly helped Buck's image as a writer. Buck Flogging's Johnson grows a little bit with each review that both he and I receive. Another few hundred reviews and Buck will be able to throw that thing over his shoulder like a scarf.

Some strategies that I've used to get reviews lately in particular have put me on a hot review-getting streak that more than amply qualifies me to write this book.

Yeah, I'm kiiinnnddd of a big deal.

Sorry, that was a pretty 2009 thing to say. Buck has always been stuck in the past. He still rocks those hot pink stretchy spandex shorts under stone-washed denim (with elastic waist) from back when Andre Agassi had Fabio hair. Wow, this must be really awkward for you right now if you don't know what I'm talking about. Holy crap, I just browsed through some pictures on the web and remembered that I had the matching Nike shoes. Today is a good day.

Also added to my resumé is:

1. I have a degree in writing. Like a real degree from a University. I know right?

2. I operate a quasi-publishing company called Archangel Ink that has helped dozens of indie authors sell more books. By dozens I mean like 14. Hey, cut me some slack. We've only been in business since November of 2013

3. I have self-published 17 books and have had two titles published by a "real" publishing company (those titles have been my poorest-performing books of all by the way).

4. I'm also an avid book narrator, with ten books of my own in audiobook format and around 20 others with another half dozen or more hitting Audible every month.

5. I'm an online entrepreneur who has started three businesses that make more money each month than the total sum I spent to launch them.
6. I'm probably the coolest person on earth. Women adore me and men want to be me.
7. My books would all be half as long if I didn't waste so much time trying to be considerably funnier than I am in real life.
8. I don't like lists all that much, but once I get started on them I have trouble stopping until I reach at least ten items.
9. Don't worry we're almost there.
10. Okay, we can move on now.

You must all be channeling Billy Madison by now, saying "Reading is good. Can we please start the story now?"

Yes we can my friends. And we shall. Hold on tight. You don't want to get bucked off.

10
Becoming a Reviewperstar

First of all, let's get real. Unlike Buck Flogging, reviews are not that big of a deal. They are important, but on the list of importance, getting lots of good reviews is actually not that close to the top. I won't risk starting another 10-item list. I'll just say that the most important things are to build an audience, do some networking with peers in your niche, write a great book with real value, choose a title very wisely, make sure your cover looks like it was made by a professional graphic designer, launch and price your book correctly, be genuine, write a good book description, put calls to action in your book, and publish often. If you do those things, you will succeed, and you'll probably get more reviews in the process.

Crap, that was 10 items. Shoulda made a list.

But most authors, and I'm as guilty as they come, have an unnecessary infatuation with reviews in proportion to their overall importance. Yes, they certainly help you to sell more books, especially as an indie author. They make you look like you can piss with the big boys. They give book browsers that tiny extra bit of confidence that can help them take the plunge and read a book by someone they've never heard of before: you.

So I don't want to say they aren't important. They are. They are key to the long-term relevance of the books you publish and your overall status and reputation as an author.

Okay, I'm glad I got that off my chest. Now we can obsessively indulge in our irrational and unjustifiable review addictions together! We, as authors, are by nature some of the most shallow and egotistical of all beings. And we are delicate little flowers, too. One bad review and we can feel our pulse rate start to rise and the force of gravity double as we slump over in our chairs.

"Hmmphfff. Das not fay-yer! I didn't say that in the book! I'm complaining to Amazon! Was this review helpful to you? Hell no! Hey honey, log into your Amazon account and vote this review down. We'll show that sonuvahbitch!"

Oh don't pretend like I'm the only one who does this. Certainly I'm not the only one who hits the refresh button 137 times per day and has a completely unhealthy obsession with the number of reviews I get. We're authors. That's just what we do. We're petty, overreacting, pointless creatures on a quest to give our lives meaning by telling everyone else how to live theirs.

Okay, we're not that bad, but it's easy to develop some bad habits. Review obsession is probably one of them, but hopefully you can transcend that, get more reviews using some of the strategies in this book, and eventually get so many that you start ignoring them.

It is natural to want you and your book to appear legit though, and nothing makes a book seem more impressive than a large number of reviews. No one else can see the sales figures behind the scenes. Sure, Amazon shows the sales rank, but few non-authors shopping for books pay much attention to that, and sales rank is but a snapshot. It's really just us authors that quickly scroll down the page to see a book's sales rank—often so quickly that the whole page freezes up.

So yes, let's admit that getting reviews is as much a matter of pride and reputation as it is about getting mo' money. I will help you get more of them, and you'll feel more successful even if your book sales don't change at all (although they probably will go up a little).

I just wanted to say before we get started, that reviews aren't everything. Don't let your life revolve around them—either the quantity or the quality, which is even less significant unless no one is saying anything good about your book. Actually, my best-selling book by far has the worst rating. Only 4.0 stars currently. Authors take note!

Don't believe me? Look at romance author Lexi Maxxwell as a case study. As I write this, Lexi prides herself on her incredible average star rating of 4.9. Impressive. None of my books have that high of an average rating. And she gets a lot of them, too. I also hardly have ANY books that sell as few copies as hers! Based on her sales rankings, none of her 34 books sell more than one copy per day despite 50+ 5-star reviews on many of her tittles, I mean titles.

She does have quite a novel system for farming out reviews though, I give her that. Check it out at http://www.leximaxxwell.com/get-me-wet/. I hope that pays off someday. Right now it doesn't appear to be. And no I don't actually read her books. I heard about her in Sean Platt and Johnny B. Truant's pretty good but excessively long (and not as cool as Buck's) book *Write. Publish. Repeat.*

So, keeping in mind that reviews aren't everything, I will now indulge your compulsion to get buttloads of them. You will be a Reviewperstar soon. Read on…

Before we do let me warn you that the 12 strategies discussed are in order of awesomeness for the most part. Don't get bored after the first few. They get better.

Review Strategy 1: Build a Following

Unlike women when Buck walks into a room, building a following isn't quick and easy. Well, that joke didn't work out quite like I wanted it to. Buck drives the ladies wild okay. That's just all you need to know.

I started publishing content online in the form of a blog (cringe, gasp, facepalm, vomit) at the end of 2006. It took me two years just to build up enough of a following to bother selling books to that following, and three more to actually make some real money doing it—real money defined as enough to pay all of my bills without my credit card balances getting larger.

So yeah, go out there and build that following tigers! It's only a half-decade away!

Buck is being facetious. Actually, achieving financial independence from scratch in five years is a remarkable feat in the real world, but on the internet it really shouldn't take that long. You probably should hop to it with a realistic timeframe in the back of your mind. Real success almost always takes years.

Knowing what I know now; however, I could go back in time and do it in two or less if I had to, which thankfully I don't. You'll certainly see Buck reach the point of selling over a thousand books per month in less time if he decides to keep writing, and that's without leveraging any of the fan base that I originally built for my other work. Buck is pretty awesome no doubt, but most literate people can do that, too, if that is what they are determined to do.

Anyway, building up a following is an essential tool—the most important tool—in getting a large quantity of gleaming reviews. It's also the hardest and most time-consuming strategy. It's not quite as effective as you think either unless you really know how to leverage it, which we'll discuss later on in the Review Team chapter.

Take for example a book I released just the other day. It was a short book on a niche topic, so not something that all my fans and followers were tripping over each other to read. I sent out this email to my subscriber list of 11,500 people, and also mentioned it to 10,000 on Facebook and 12,500 Twitter followers:

"I decided to go ahead and release my latest, short book:

Now, you know I'm a fool for you guys, trying to give you every sliver of information and entertainment I have in me for absolutely no cost to you whatsoever. But to keep being able to give you guys free content, new releases especially, I do need just a wee tiny bit of reciprocation if you can bear it.

It goes kind of like this:

1. Give away everything to loyal subscribers for free
2. Get lots of downloads and reviews to establish my book on Amazon
3. Sell that book to people who aren't my loyal peeps
4. ~~Buy groceries~~ Order pizza and rent 80's movies

Steps 3 and 4 can't happen without Step 2, and if Step 2 doesn't happen, then I can't continue my Step 1 habit. And to be honest, this whole free book thingee has been delightful on all fronts for everyone involved. I really want to keep it going.

So please, download the book. Read this short, little book, and when you're done with it, please take a moment to give it a nice review. To properly establish this thing, I'm looking for 100+ reviews if you guys have got it in ya.

Thanks and enjoy the book.

If you don't have an eReader or tablet, that's okay. You can read it right on your computer screen by Downloading Kindle Cloud Reader. https://read.amazon.com"

You would think with a following like that receiving a notification of a free book, being asked very creatively to review the thing, and 4,000 downloads in the first 35 hours, that I would have gotten those 100 reviews by now. Just 34 so far. I'm not complaining. Most that downloaded it probably haven't read the thing yet in order to review it. I'm sure over the next week I will come dangerously close to 100 reviews. It may go on to become the third book to enter the 100 club.

Okay, the more I think about it the more pleased I am. I won't whine anymore. I will, to be certain, refresh the page for it on Amazon 462 times between now and that 100th review.

Man, I'm sounding like such a little spoiled diva. A year ago every time I got a review I was all like: http://www.youtube.com/watch?v=k4SU169RFJ8

So yes, please build up a following, and don't blog to do it! For chrissakes man, you're an author! Have some dignity! You can read about some of Buck's unbeatable author strategies for building a following without blogging your life away in his almost-as-awesome-as-*Reviewperstar* book, *Kill Your Blog*.

Review Strategy 2: Write a Good Book

Now, I know that YOU don't write fluffy meaningless crap and then publish it on Amazon. That's what other people do. Yet, Amazon is overrun with crappy books written by brainless and spineless douchebags that don't help, enlighten, or entertain anyone. So someone must be writing these books, which is why Buck needs to tell everyone to make sure their books are actually worth reading.

When you write a good book, you will inspire a certain percentage of readers to take a moment to review the thing. They will simply feel the need to talk about how excited they are and use Amazon as a sounding board.

If your book is really bad you'll also get a lot of reviews bashing the thing. The internet has brought about a radical new degree of honesty in human-to-human communication. Get ready to be brutalized unmercifully if your book is crap, especially if Buck reads it. Dude'll lay into you like a sleeping bag.

I don't have any major tips or wisdom to give you on writing good books other than the following (oh shit, a list):

1. **Write a lot.** Practice makes better. If you're not capable of writing a really good book right now, that's okay. Write the thing anyway. Nothing will get you to write more, practice more, and get better at it faster than writing books. My first book sucked. I cringe when I try to read it now, but I've gotten better for no other reason than the fact that I've done a lot of it. And if the thing gets shredded with bad reviews or doesn't sell much at all? Doesn't matter. Throwing yourself into the ring is a better way to learn how to fight than reading a book about how to do it and throwing your first punch at the heavyweight champ. As you write better books, simply unpublish the crap that came before it. I've pulled six books down with a total of around 250,000 words. It wasn't a waste. It made me the human version of a light saber that I am today. You'll get faster at writing, too, which is important for the next tip…

2. **Binge write.** This may not work for you, but I doubt it. It works great for me, and I can't imagine writing any other way: go on a writing binge. Immersing yourself in a book from the time the first word is written until the last word is written is the ultimate way to write a good, coherent book with good flow and little repetition. When you just write a little here and there, picking at the thing for an hour once a week, it takes a lot of time to get back into the zone. You spend more time getting back into the flow than you do in the flow. Live and breathe a book when you write it. Work on it at least for a couple of hours every day until a full draft is complete. The longest I've ever spent writing even a full-length book is one month, and the fewer total days I take to get it done the better it comes out. Then I take a few weeks off or longer to revise the thing, start researching and thinking about what I want to write next, and otherwise recharge my mental batteries by laying around like dirty laundry watching Youtube and hitting the refresh button 876 times a day. Book writing should be like sex. Once you start, think about as

little as possible outside of getting it done right, and don't stop until you're finished. You may work 50 hours a week at your real job (real job, lol), but there's still plenty of time to sit down at night and write for a couple hours after dinner every night and extra on the weekends. If you would rather watch TV than write, you probably should just watch it. A real writer can't help but write and gets off by doing it. Buck is not even wearing pants right now as he types this. He's actually procrastinating by writing right now. He's got a business launching in ten days and started writing this book to put off all the less fun stuff he's got to do before it goes live.

3. **Revise, edit, and proofread**. Take this process very seriously. Most people say that authors are not very good at editing their own stuff. To some extent, this is true. Your writing will always sound better to you than it does to others unless you have really low self-esteem. Buck has no problem in that department. What I've found is that having others edit your work helps you become a better self-editor. When a really good editor works on your "perfect" manuscript and tears it apart, you realize after a period of shouting, drunkenness, and beating

inanimate objects that you are actually pretty sloppy and stupid. When you realize this, you get better. So have someone point out your bad habits. At some point you may be able to edit your own work. If not, at least the editor's job will get easier as you improve with each round of "Doh, I can't believe I wrote that." I've found that the less I need an editor, the more I seek them out. The "that's good enough" attitude held me back for many years, but I've gotten to the point now where I can admit that my writing isn't perfect, and that many things could use some rephrasing. I catch typos pretty well though, mostly because I read so effing slow. Most people recommend that indie authors go to a service like http://www.paper-perfect-editing.com. I just checked prices, and that's tough to justify unless you know you're sitting on a gold mine. As soon as you can afford it, do it. I'd be willing to do a light editing and proofreading job on a nonfiction book for cheap if you can't find anyone else. For inquiries regarding that, send an email to: buck@archangelink.com

Man, I so probably should have extended this list to 10 items with 7 totally ridiculous things on it.

That would have been funny. But what did you spend, less than $7 on this? Hey, you get what you pay for lady. I'm moving on to the next chapter. Oh, but before I do, here is an interesting case study for you. I just helped a couple of guys launch their brand-new books for free. Both started with zero reviews of course, and both got almost the exact same number of downloads, making it to #1 in their respective categories in Amazon's free store. Here's the screen shot taken at the same time and placed side by side:

Best Sellers in **Cookbooks, Food & Wine**   Best Sellers in **Health, Fitness & Dieting**
Top 100 Paid   Top 100 Free   Top 100 Paid   Top 100 Free

1. Chocolate at Home: How to Make your o...
by Ben Hirshberg
★★★★★ (5)
Kindle Edition
Free

1. Whole Grains, Empty Promises: The Sur...
by Anthony Colpo
★★★★★ (17)
Kindle Edition
Free

Now that both have been out for 10 days now, the one on the left has 9 reviews and the one on the right has 28 reviews. Same number of downloads, and only three of the 37 total reviews are less than 5 stars. So what's the difference? Primarily the difference is the quality of the book, the subject matter, and the size of the pre-built audience.

The dude on the right has been writing all over the internet for nearly a decade, and is an incredibly meticulous writer and researcher laying down some really groundbreaking stuff. His writing style is incredible as well—a literary assassin.
The book on the left, while good and getting good reviews, doesn't have the same punch, nor does Ben have a big following. The subject matter is a little fluffier as well. This is just an example of the difference between a book that leverages strategies 1 and 2 vs. a book that doesn't. In this case it's more than a 300% difference in reviewperstardom.

Review Strategy 3: Keep it Short

I'm such a dork. A woman wrote me a review today and said, and I quote, "I wish it would have been longer!" And I actually, really, not-making-this-up wrote, "That's what she said!"

I'm *that* hilarious. Really.

I wouldn't want to deter you from writing a full-length book, especially if it's a fiction book. From what I understand, people reading fiction books really expect to get 80,000 words for $2.99 if you're an indie author. Glad I don't write fiction. That's like writing six books for the price of one.

In nonfiction, the best strategy as of 2014 is to write a lot of short books and price them cheaper than what's being published by real publishing companies. I don't know any author writing about self-publishing these days that would disagree.

Strictly from a review-getting point of view with no other factors considered, writing a short book will always pull more reviews than a longer book, simply by virtue of the fact that far more people are likely to read the whole thing. The more people that finish a book, the more book reviews you are likely to receive. There is a big difference in a 10,000-word book's ability to get reviews compared to a 50,000-word book. Simple as that.

Those reviews also seem to come in faster. That's not that big of a deal, but it is nice to know that running a free promo for five days will give me a book with double-digit reviews by the end of the first week.

I also envision the reader getting to the end and not feeling exhausted, having a little energy left over to go write a quick review when I suggest (code word for beg, shame, and command) that they do so.

I also envision the reader being slightly dissatisfied with the length (Buck never leaves anyone dissatisfied with his length; guy's got a damn shin-bruiser hanging from his shorts), and wanting to voice their yearning for more in the review section.

Maybe that's a stretch, but write a really short book, and you'll see what I'm talking about. Calculate the number of reviews against the number of downloads and sure enough, shorty gets stars. Buck's first book has had 24 reviews thus far with no promotion or pleading for review-writing in just

910 downloads. That's 1 for every 38 downloads, and that's with just two of the following strategies! I have a 60,000-word book with nearly 8,000 downloads that I asked over 1,000 people to kindly review. It's only got four more than Buck's *Kill Your Blog* right now!

I wouldn't re-arrange your whole writing career to write short books strictly to get more reviews, but if you're on the fence about whether to split up that 40,000-word book into four short ones instead of one long one, take this simple fundamental of review fetching into account.

Review Strategy 4: Call for Review

This is a little thing, but it makes a big difference. It's little tricks like this that make this book worth reading. Well, Buck's relentless sense of humor and sexual innuendo makes this book worth reading. Information like this is just a bonus.

Simple enough really—let your readers know at the end of each book that they are really helping you out by taking a few minutes to write a review.

You'll see at the end of this book that there is a call for review. Because of the nature of this book, it's written a little differently. But ultimately, something like this is what I've found to be the most effective so far:

"Last but not least, please write a short, helpful review of this book if it helped you (or at least entertained you) in any way. As a writer, I live and die by the quantity and quality of the reviews I receive. You've no doubt received this book at a great price and received good value that will have

an impact on your future. Please return the favor. It will only take a few minutes of your time. You can do that HERE."

Of course, HERE is hyperlinked to where they can write a review for that particular book. Also, be sure to give this call for review its very own page with a title like: Help Me Out, or I Have a Small Favor to Ask or something along those lines.

It seems people are moved most by knowing that they can do something to help another person out. I know I am that way. Buck is moved most by large, round booties covered in baby oil, but he is a very unique individual with very different values. Most readers don't really know that reviews not only help an author be more successful, but also make the author *feel* more successful, which is of equal if not greater importance if we were to really analyze the thing to death (don't worry, we won't).

If readers like your book, and even more importantly, they like YOU, this kind of call to action is very effective. I obviously put a lot of personality into my books and evoke strong feelings in readers. I tend to get a lot of strong positive, and strong negative reviews, and a lot in a general sense because of that. Don't be scared by those negative reviews either. My bestselling book (by far, #1 in its category for 15 straight months now), has a whopping 28, 1-star reviews, and 14, 2-star reviews right now.

I was scared at first, thinking that such reviews would hurt my sales, but ultimately the

100+ 5-star reviews have greatly overshadowed the negatives, and my sales rank just keeps getting better and better as each month passes. Most of the negative reviews are just a bunch of religious fanatics bitching about completely benign words in the book like "douche." I think that even strengthens the compulsion to buy when all of the negatives are putting more emphasis on the word choices than the solidity of the content.

I also run a lot of free promotions as we'll discuss in the next chapter, and when I do I crank the call for review up another notch by pointing out that the book was free, and that the reader owes it to me for giving away my hard work and valuable insights for nothing. Right now I'm running a free book with a page at the end that says:

A Small Favor to Ask

"How did you like your free book? I hope you liked it. And I hoped you liked getting it for free!

It's my pleasure to give you books at absolutely no cost. I hope to continue to do so with my future book releases, but I need a small favor from all of you who enjoyed this book—please write a short review on Amazon. As an author, I depend on a large quantity of quality reviews for my books. Please do it right now before you forget and get busy with something else. It will only take a few minutes of your time and will help me out more than you can imagine. You can do that HERE."

Another thought I've had, although I haven't tried it, is to sort of use the YouTube comment strategy in your call to review. You've seen that right? Where a vlogger will ask a question and tell the viewers to leave their comments or answers below? I thought of maybe asking them to answer a question in their review, like "In your review, tell me what topic you would like me to write about next, and the topic with the most votes will become my next book." I don't know if it would work or not, but think about it some. You might come up with a real crotch-rocking idea that sends 'em piling into the review section.

Anyway, the call for review at the end helps. I haven't studied enough to know exactly how much, but my quantity of reviews has skyrocketed in the last several months, so I know I'm doing something right. I'm doing several somethings right, and this is surely one of them. I know it's easy to just say "screw it," but do it and they will review it. There's nothing to it.

Review Strategy 5: KDP Select

I've tried lots of things as an author. I've listed books on Kobo, Google Play, Lulu, and Barnes and Noble. I've sold my books on my site as eBooks and audiobooks. I've sold book bundles and participated in book bundles. But ultimately, mother Amazon was always the kindest. Instead of spreading myself out, I decided to concentrate all my efforts towards performing well at the world's best bookseller: I enrolled all of my self-published books in KDP Select.

With KDP Select, the eBook version of your book must only be for sale in Amazon's Kindle store—nowhere else. It's a bummer because I did get some sales from all of those other vendors, sometimes up to $600-700 per month. I can't say I fully make that up by listing my eBooks only on Kindle, but what I have done is simplify the process and save myself a whole lot of coordinating and orchestrating and headache. Plus, I just like Amazon. Screw all them other fools.

When you enroll in KDP Select, you are awarded certain advantages that other authors cannot take advantage of. The privileges of the KDP Select program speak volumes about what really works to help books sell better with the way Amazon's algorithm is set up. The two main benefits are:

1. You get to give your book away for free for 5 days out of every 90. Giving away your book for free is an advantage that helps your book sell? It sounds strange I know, but the answer is yes.

2. Or you can instead opt to drop the price way down below Amazon's royalty basement of $2.99 and still get a 70% royalty rate (normal authors get 35%), and run a "Countdown Deal" on the thing. I won't go into detail about this, but it's an amazing tool, and authors are raving about it right now. They're raving about it perhaps a little too much, as they're calling free promotions "dead." For more, read Steve Scott's *Is $.99 the New Free?*

Among many of Buck's talents has been raising free promotions from the dead. The guy is like Jesus, or maybe like Aura from *Flash Gordon*—

except Buck doesn't bring back blonde Jets quarterbacks from the dead. No sir. Well, he might do that for Tebow. He does miss that Tebow.

Here's how it works:

On an average free promotion through my real list of followers and subscribers I get about 10,000 free downloads for each 5-day free promotion. As I mentioned earlier, Buck was getting an incredible 1 review for every 38 downloads. If I could somehow find him a way to get 10,000 downloads like I can on my others, that would be an incredible 263 reviews—263 for giving away my book for just 5 days out of 90. How do you think those reviews would affect the other 85 days? Reviews aren't everything like I said, but 263 can certainly sell an extra five days' worth of books every three months. That I know for sure.

If I ran a free promo at that rate the maximum four times per year, I might get up to 1,000 reviews in a single year. How would those 20 free days affect my ability to sell that book for the following 5 years? You catching my drift here sailor?

Let's not forget that every time I got 10,000 downloads I'm cross-promoting other books of mine and selling considerably more of those books.

Also think about building hundreds of reviews on several books in your library. What does that do for your reputation and status in the eye of the prospective buyer when viewing your author page? What if a big-time publishing company saw that page? Think they might contact you for a big publishing deal? I bet they would. I still wouldn't recommend saying yes unless they are paying a big advance, but still, it's cool when that happens.

Yes, one of the great keys to getting reviews is getting more downloads. KDP Select's free promotion allows you to get exponentially more downloads than you would selling the thing—even for 99 cents. More downloads, more reviews.

I will say that your book better be pretty solid and professional if you are going to do this. People who get free books give reviews that are notoriously more negative than the reviews you get from people who already know, like, and read your work. Again, I honestly think quantity matters at least twice as much as quality unless you're averaging less than 3.8 stars. At that point, it probably will hurt your sales. You will really have to screw up a book to get that low of a rating though. If you do, that's fine. At least you learned that you can get better and work on improving your game. Worst-case scenario is that you have to pull the book down, improve it, and re-release it.

So the overall verdict?

KDP Select free promos get a big nod of approval from Buck. While he's just started testing the waters with this strategy, it looks like his total reviews over time, if he sticks with this strategy and keeps a long-term vision in mind for the success of his book, will be astronomically high.

Keep in mind that I in no way can promise or want to lead you to believe that you can get 10,000 free downloads per promotion or reviews at a rate of 1 for every 38 downloads. Realistically, you can expect more like 500-1000 downloads if you are a new author with maybe 1 out of every 100 downloads if you are extremely lucky and utilize several tips from this book. That's only 5-10 reviews. After four promotions in one year however, that could be 20-40, which is what most authors consider to be enough to move a book—selling several copies per day.

Still, it's a viable strategy, and an even more viable strategy when you have an audience built up that can propel every free book you run to the top of the kindle free store for thousands of extra downloads. It's something every author should be aware of and take carefully into consideration, especially if you have plans of making writing your sole career.

Review Strategy 6: TwiggleFace+ Tricks

Buck used to think that social networks weren't helpful for getting many reviews. Then one day he did something that really helped. It hit him completely by surprise: he posted a really bad review of one of his books on Facebook.

The review was 1-star. Here it is right here:

1 of 25 people found the following review helpful

★☆☆☆☆ **It is really bad don't get this book!!! It will ruin your life dont do it!**, December 2, 2013

By **Steven** - See all my reviews

Amazon Verified Purchase (What's this?)

This review is from: **Diet Recovery 2: Restoring Mind and Metabolism from Dieting, Weight Loss, Exercise, and Healthy Food (Kindle Edition)**

This Book really sucks No one ever read it It si not as good as it is said to be and Matt stone is not a good writer

Help other customers find the most helpful reviews   Report abuse | Permalink
Was this review helpful to you? [Yes] [No]   Comment (1)

I posted this thing on Facebook, and people went nuts. Not only did they rush over to vote the review down as unhelpful as you can see, but this triggered a flurry of 5-Star reviews from loyal fans of mine that came unglued at such a review. I think it led to 13 new reviews in about 48 hours to counter this one. It also provided good entertainment, with endless comments and likes on the post.

I wasn't a turd about it at all, just pointed out how enthusiastic I was about being called a bad writer by someone with minimal grasp on the skill. I celebrated it in fact, and today it remains as the only 1-star review out of 93 currently. I figured this was a sign that I actually am a pretty good writer, and even better at figuring out which letters to capitalize and where to place the proper punctuation.

Of course, an opportunity like this doesn't come along too often, and you have to build up somewhat of an audience on the social media outlet of your choice to possibly get any real reviews from it. But it worked for me, and I'm not exactly a social media dynamo. I think I had about 6,500 Facebook likes on my fan page at the time this stellar review was posted.

I have also posted good reviews for people to go check out, which is good social proof, and it inspired a few others to share their thoughts in the form of a review—also voting up the good review to be seen by more book browsers.

Some other posts that helped fetch some reviews were screenshots of how my new releases were performing in their categories shortly after release. If you've released a book for cheap to a pre-built audience, you know that your book quickly floats to the top of the ranks—making your dick (male or female) look about 12 feet long.

The same book above was released at just 99 cents, which triggered 1800 sales in 48 hours. This was enough to propel it all the way to the #1 Hot New Release in all of nonfiction. While I didn't get a screenshot of that, it was a huge victory for my fans to see my book alongside of my nemesis, Jillian Michaels. She writes books about how to diet. I write books about the negatives of dieting and how to recover from them physically and psychologically. This screenshot posted on Facebook made my fans nearly wet themselves, and galvanized them to fight the evil diet mistress of the universe with glowing review after glowing review.

This is by no means a strategy that you should solely rely on or count on to deliver a substantial number of reviews. But for a total of about 15 minutes of work and 4-5 social media posts, it has delivered at least 25 reviews, lots of up and down voting, and much fun. What I like the most about this strategy in particular is that I didn't ask anyone for a review to get them. Asking for reviews gets tiring, coming off spammy over time even when giving free books away. So this strategy is a little gem, but still a gem. I will certainly be using it in the future when opportunities like the above present themselves.

Review Strategy 7: Email Signature

I haven't tried this one yet—not because it wouldn't work. In fact, with the way my business works this could potentially be the most effective strategy of all. I haven't tried it because my email is unorganized, and I respond to people about several different businesses all out of one account. But if I just had a writing business, all published under one name, well then, this would be a doozie of a review net.

I say this because I take a ton of time to personally answer tons of reader emails. When I say tons, I mean tons. I have probably taken the time to carefully read and thoughtfully answer 5,000 emails over the last half decade. If only I would have had a little something in my signature area that called them for a review.

In a perfect world, it would say something like:

"I answer dozens of reader emails just like yours every single day, because I really care about your health and well-being. If you feel served by the time I've dedicated to answering your questions free of charge, no need to get out the credit card. You can repay me by simply writing a short review of one or more of my books on Amazon. It really helps my success as an author and helps more people just like you connect with me and find the information they need. Please be courteous and take a moment to write a quick review. It will only take a few minutes of your time. You can do that HERE."

I'd link that HERE to my author page, where I'd probably get these people to not only write a review or two, but buy a book or two as well, helping me to better justify all the time spent helping them out. I like helping them out don't get me wrong, and I've built a reputation up for way over-delivering on personal care and attention to all of my fans, but I sure could use more to show for those 5,000 emails that I've written over the years.

Actually, writing this short chapter is really making me think of how I could do exactly that. It may take a little extra time, but I may test it out soon just by pasting the above call to review in communications that I deem appropriate to do so. I bet I could get at least 10-20 reviews per week from this strategy alone—that's 500-1,000 per year roughly.

Try this strategy out if you think this applies to you, and if you are getting worn down and disgruntled from answering a lot of personal emails with little reciprocation from the people you are sending these heartfelt responses to.

Review Strategy 8: Write Reviews

Call it karma, call it an act of goodwill, call it a conscience-clearer. I call it a good way to get some Amazon-specific visibility and hopefully a little reviewprocation. Write some reviews of other books.

Now, Amazon has a funny rule about authors writing reviews for competitors in their own genre. No really, you're technically not allowed to write reviews on books that compete with your own. I think they do this so that authors don't run around trying to slander each other. I've been tempted many times, especially to write some satirical reviews under a different name. But I haven't. Some close calls for sure.

Write positive, helpful reviews, and I'm sure you won't get hassled.

Being a heavy reviewer on Amazon is smart. You can make yourself a little reviewer profile and actually promote yourself subtly by virtue of the fact that a lot of quality reviews will give you a lot of exposure to Amazon-browsing eyes. You can even give yourself a little tagline so that you appear as, say, "Buck Flogging, author of *Reviewperstar*."

Even better, although it takes some courage, is to leave video reviews. Yes, few people do this (which is what makes you stand out even more), but you can actually create a video and say something like:

"Hi, I'm Buck Flogging, author of *Reviewperstar*. As an expert on the subject of writing books and a successful author myself, I found Steve Scott's book *61 Ways to Sell More Nonfiction Books* to be simply outstanding, blah, blah, blah."

Then of course you go and do what any slimeball author would do, and get all of your friends and family members to go and vote your review up so that the maximum number of book browsers see the thing. You could also send an email to Steve telling him about your review and thank him for all the great information. Steve, being the relentlessly nice guy that he is, would probably end up returning the favor to you somehow.

By the way I love ol' Steve and have narrated many of his books, mostly under his pen name S.J. Scott. His author-related books (http://www.amazon.com/Steve-Scott/e/B0098NFKNM/) *are* very helpful.

Anyway, I won't dwell on this. You get the point. Go write or record some great, heartfelt reviews on <u>new</u> books, vote your review up to the top, and let thousands of people see it as it stands out as the first, most prominent and "helpful" review in the lot for all eternity. Don't be too promotional. Don't be promotional at all beyond casually mentioning who you are.

You can start this act of goodwill when you are done reading this book. Right? Guys?

You can read more about this in E.T. Barton's book about getting more reviews. Right now she has more spelling errors in the book than she has reviews, but there is some decent information in that book, including links to a review-trading group that she manages, and the lady likes Roller Derby. She also describes herself as slutty. Buck is sold. Buck loves slutty, hardcore Roller Derby biatches. Buck always turns the B word into a 3-syllable affair.

Seriously though, E.T. Barton's review-trading group is a great way to get reviews written for writing reviews, which is what makes this a viable strategy deserving placement amongst the big 12.

Review Strategy 9: Audible Discount Codes

I'm an Audible fanatic. I don't mean I actually listen to audiobooks. Good heavens, no. Believe it or not, I don't even own a phone. Straight Skypetarian these days and living the dream at $4.99/month.

I guess some people love these things, and the number of some people that love these things is growing at a shocking rate.

I sold 110 audiobooks in December. I sold 155 in January. I sold 263 in February.

One of my audiobook clients made over $1,000 his first month live with no promotion, which is almost exactly what he makes from the Kindle and paperback versions of his book per month combined! He's an 83-year old man who knows diddley about all things electronic. Yet he's obliterating Audible. Today he was ranked #22 in a category with 3,400 titles—one slot behind Dale

Carnegie and having his way with Jack Canfield, Tony Robbins, Leo Babauta, and Vaynerchuk. All he did was send me a manuscript and $1,000, and now he's making more per month than he paid to get in the game.

You heard it here first. Audible is the new Kindle. Audible is the new frontier. With its bounty program and affiliate program and all its other bonuses and such, I actually made over $9 per copy sold on a book priced at $6.95 in November. At Audible, the impossible happens.

I'm not just saying that because I make money narrating people's books. In kind of a messed up roundabout way I actually don't make any money doing it. I narrate people's books because the opportunities there are endless, and most indie authors have been conditioned to believe that audiobooks just "aren't worth it" or are "out of reach." That's just not so, and short nonfiction books in particular are relentlessly successful due to the low cost of production and low price of the audiobook. Hear me now, believe me later!

If anything, I started narrating audiobooks to help authors seize these lost opportunities. The audiobook game is so much bigger than authors realize.

Anyway, that whole infomercial aside, Audible reviews and ratings are proving extremely difficult to get, but because there is so much potential there, it's absolutely worth taking advantage of their free review copies.

When you upload a book to ACX, an Amazon platform that lists your book on Audible, Amazon, and iTunes for you, you can request 25 discount codes that you can give away as "review copies." Please do this, and use some of the upcoming "Review Team" strategies to make sure that a high rate of people that you give these copies to are game for writing a review, or at the very least rating the thing.

If you have even the tiniest following you should have no problem giving away 25 free copies of an audiobook and getting a handful of good reviews and ratings to establish the thing. I'm pissed that I just found out about these codes after having already made and promoted six audiobooks! But I won't make that mistake again with the two I've got coming out in March, including this one.

Speaking of free review copies, if you would like to listen to Buck's book *Kill Your Blog*, there are still a few review codes left. Send an email to: elizabeth@180degreehealth.com and tell her you'd like a free Audible review code for it. She'll send you one if there are any left. But you better rate and review that thing when you're done, or Buck will come after you. 19-inch biceps. Nuff said.

B.D.P Strategies

Review Strategy 10: Build a Review Team

Now it's time to talk about some real heavy-hitter review strategies here. As far as Amazon is concerned, it's cool to offer a review copy to someone in exchange for a review. As long as you aren't paying them to write a review, it's kosher. They do state in their rules that a reviewer should plainly state that he or she received a review copy—making that publicly known.

Also, those reviews will not be listed as being a "verified purchase," but that doesn't make much of a difference to a book browser. Most book shoppers don't pay much attention to such a thing. Anyway, with a big audience eager to eat up my book releases, I was able to leverage that to the extreme.

The book that I unleashed this strategy upon was published by a formal publishing company, so I really wanted to make sure that I:

1. Overwhelmed them with the number of reviews I could generate, and indeed I did. They reported that our review list was twice as big as the next largest list they have ever received, and we're talking about a publishing company that has put out a half dozen NY Times bestsellers over the past few years.
2. Didn't waste their money. I was horrified that they would spend thousands of dollars, and that my people wouldn't actually deliver on the review-writing they had agreed upon.

So the following is how my partner Rob and I pulled off the unthinkable. We got 248 reviews in just a few short weeks, all from sending out 288 review copies. That's right, only 40 out of 288 complete strangers received their review copy and failed to read it and quickly write up a review for it. Amazing. I can't believe it went so well, and I owe it all to Mr. Rob Archangel, an angel indeed.

While it may be a bit overkill, I wanted to show you the exact communications that were sent out originally to 600 people that requested a review copy. We had to narrow that list down only to those who were really game to follow through. In other words, we used the following communications to filter down the list.

I'm sure that will be of great importance to

you, because mailing out physical review copies of a book is farking expensive—nearly $10 per copy for the publisher I'm certain. So if you're in essence paying someone $10 for a review, you better be damn sure that person is actually going to write a review!

Physical copies are nice to send out, but there are much cheaper ways to go about doing this that have the added bonus of counting as a sale and bumping up your rankings. We'll discuss that in the next chapter though.

For now, here's Rob to walk you through the lengthy communication process that got us such incredible review results. With a title you know is destined to greatness and worthy of some up-front expenditures to catapult it to the top of the marketplace, this strategy is definitely worthy of your consideration…

Hey everyone, Rob here. When Buck opened the floodgates announcing that we'd make available a free paperback copy of Solving the Paleo Equation *available for advance review, I woke up to literally hundreds of emails. I knew I had to find a way to cull the herd a bit, and make sure that everyone who replied was fully on board. So I drafted a somewhat intimidating, but still energetic email that I used as a template to reply to everyone who was writing to request a copy. Since not everyone was replying to the broadcast to the newsletter (we also mentioned it over*

Facebook), I included Matt's email below mine for context. Here's what I wrote:

First Email

Thanks for your interest!

As Matt mentioned in the email that went out (copied below), **these copies are for advance *review,* and we really need everyone to commit to spreading the word if you receive a copy.** Much as we are hip to just spread the love, these are spiffy paperback titles sent out directly from the publisher, and they cannot just sit on your bookshelf when you get one. Here's what we need you to agree to:

1. **You will set aside time to read through the book when it arrives and write a reasonably thoughtful review on Amazon, social media, YouTube, your personal blog, email newsletter, etc., and it has to be published between January 1 and January 10, 2014** (a few days before would be ok too, but no later than Jan 10th).

2. No need to go Charles Dickens with a 3,000 word analysis (though you're welcome to if you like!), and certainly be honest, whether you love it or hate it. But please don't just post "This book was cool" on your Facebook wall and be done with it. The more avenues of honest exposure the better, but Amazon reviews probably carry the most weight if you can only select one.

3. **You *have* to send me a link to your review.** Could be on any one or more of those avenues listed above and the more the better. If you somehow get it into print, awesome! But send me a scanned image of it if there's not an online URL to direct me to.

4. I'll be keeping track of everyone's review, and may accost you as often as every day starting January 1 until I get a link to yours. After I get it, I'll quit bugging you, but until then, expect frequent reminders about this agreement.

If you can't commit to this, no worries. It's coming up on holiday time, everyone is busy and it's all good. But we ask that you hold off on this offer. **We need 100% of you to follow through, so take a moment and assess whether this will be right for you.**

If you're certain you're up for the task and can agree to all this, **Please reply back to me with the subject line "I agree" and the following information in the email body** (even if you've sent it already):

- Full name
- Mailing address
- Country
- Your website (if you have one)
- Email address
- Phone number (if international)

- **Which avenues you intend to post your review on**

Send this no later than 5 pm NY time Dec 7, 2013 and I'll put you on the list. **Emails not following this format may slip through the cracks, so please include the subject line and information above.** You should get the copy in the next week or two barring any unforeseen changes or issues, which I'll follow up with you about if they arise.

To those of you confirming from outside the US, I'll also follow up with you if we're able to send review copies your way.

Thanks for your interest. We'd love to see this reach to the top of the charts, and help lots of people, and your efforts will go a long way toward that.

I look forward to your confirmation,
Rob
PS: **One more mention- 100% follow through, cool?**

Matt's email

Big news everyone! My next book (co-authored with Dr. Garrett Smith who just wrote an article in the first issue of the *180 Newsletter*), published by Victory Belt, is coming out in less than a month! I just spoke to the publisher yesterday, and he said that they are willing to ship out **FREE** copies wherever I want them to go. And I want them to go to as many of you as possible!

Now, these are going to be advance copies for review. These are really nice books that will retail at more than $21. So this is not necessarily just a kind offer to send some books out. In order to get a copy mailed out to you, you must be willing to write a review on Amazon, on a blog if you have one, post about it on social media networks, or all of the above.

And these reviews will need to be posted roughly between January 1st and January 10th. If this sounds like something you would be interested in, send an email to: rob@180degreehealth.com with your name and mailing address. Please reply by no later than Saturday of this week.

Not sure if the publisher will mail out copies outside of the U.S., but it's worth a try if you are interested.

The book is called *Solving the Paleo Equation: Stress, Nutrition, Exercise, Sleep*. Below is a little bit about it. Enjoy the book! And like our STPE page on Facebook https://www.facebook.com/solvingthepaleoequation

---

Rob Commentary

As you see, I included very specific instructions on how to reply to me, as I outlined below. Details like name, contact information, outlets one planned to post this review on, etc. had to be included, and I requested a separate email. This made things easier for me organizationally, and created a bar for prospective reviewers to hurdle over. It was a small bar, but the goal was to get them invested, however slightly, in this process and following through.

I did have some people who didn't comply and did my best to work with them. But many others (dozens) simply never followed up after this initial email to get put on our reviewer list. And that was fine- we were happy to make sure that those we sent books two knew exactly what was expected, and can follow basic guidelines.

About a week after the deadline, I sent the below follow up email out.

Second Email

Greetings everyone,

If you're receiving this email, you have requested an advance review copy of the new book by Dr. Garrett Smith and Matt Stone, *Solving the Paleo Equation*. You've read through my email and taken a sworn oath that you will read the book upon arrival, and post a thoughtful review about it between January 1 and January 10, 2014. You've agreed to provide me a link/screenshot/image of the reviews that you write, and you accept that I will continue to pester you until you've provided them. You've committed to this 100%, and we need each of you to follow through, no exceptions, love it or hate it.

Now… Welcome to the club!

Your contact information has been forwarded to the publisher and review copies should be sent out soon, arriving within a week or two. Here are some review guidelines:

- Although we said blogs and Facebook posts are fine outlets, I want to emphasize that Amazon is the single best place for reviews for us, unless you have a very substantial online following through your blog, Facebook page, etc. And even if you do have a big following, consider copying the body of your review to Amazon, as that is the biggest marketplace in the world for books, and a review there will be most impactful. Other book-centric venues such as Goodreads are also great, and appeal to a certain type of discerning reader. A good minimum review length to shoot for is 150 words.
- Please be HONEST. Whether you love or hate the book, or feel indifferent toward it, tell us why in a thoughtful and reflective way. The most meaningful reviews tend to be *useful,* even more than good or bad. Describe specific examples of what you did o r did not like, and why.
- Other possible aspects to the review: who do you think this book would be good for? What is your background with the subject matter and why did this book come to interest you? Did it meet your expectations?
- Address concerns some readers (or fellow reviewers) might have. It is *very* useful to other

readers when one review addresses another negative review. Take a little time reading through other reviewers' comments and consider weighing in on whether the criticism leveled was valid.

That's it!

Thank you all again for agreeing to this. We hope you enjoy the book, and that if you do, you'll be as motivated as we are to spread the word far and wide. We'd like nothing more than to see this book catapult up the ranks of the bestseller list and empower millions of people to self-design their own health game plan.

Rob

Rob Commentary

This was one more reminder of what they'd agreed to, and it provided a nice opportunity to check in.

I also used it as a platform to suggest review guidelines and get them thinking about how to craft a review. Of course, not everyone will have a stellar, 'rock my world' kind of review, but at least this provides a starting point to jump off from.

Another week or so later, after we received notice that there would be some printing delays, I sent the following email:

Third Email

Greetings and happy holidays advance reviewers of Matt Stone and Dr. Garrett Smith.

Just a brief update- some of you have written in to inquire about the status of your review copies. I was informed by our publisher that they've run into printing delays; we now expect copies to ship out the second or third week of January. If anyone needs to update their mailing address as a result of this change, please contact me ASAP, and I will make sure your correct address is on file.

Obviously since no one will have copies in time to review between January 1 and January 10, our review deadlines have shifted back. I will reach out to you all again with the new dates once we have confirmed review copy shipment.

I apologize for the delay- we're very excited to get this book out there, and were hoping to catch the post-Christmas flurry of activity. Hopefully we can still make as big a splash, just a few weeks later.

One last thing: if this revised shipping timeframe will impede your ability to provide a review, please do let me know. Several of you indicated that the holidays were going to afford you the free time necessary to commit to this before heading back to your busy schedules. If I don't hear from you, I'll assume everyone is still 100% on board to write a timely review upon receipt of their copy.

Thanks again everyone- warm regards!
Rob

Rob Commentary

Again, just another check in, and this one offering folks the chance to opt out if they were not fully on board for the review. We did have a few who backed out, but mostly everyone stayed.

When the books were sent from the warehouse to the reviewers, an adapted version of the guidelines were sent out with the below letter:

Letter Printed and Sent with Review Copies

Greetings everyone,

Thank you for your interest in this advance review copy of *Solving the Paleo Equation* by Matt Stone and Dr. Garrett Smith. You've all read through our emails and have taken a sworn oath that you will read the book upon arrival, and post a thoughtful review about it. Printing delays have advanced our timeline, but you all should receive this book by the third week of January. Allotting a week or so for reading, **please post your review between February 1 and February 10 on** Amazon.com. Once you've done that, provide Rob a link/screenshot/image of your reviews via his email address rob@180degreehealth.com

He will reach out to everyone beginning February 1, and will continue contacting you as often as every day until your review is up. You've committed to this 100%, and we need each of you to follow through, no exceptions, whether you love the book or hate it.

Now, onto some guidelines:

- Although we said blogs and Facebook posts are fine outlets, we want to emphasize that Amazon is the single best place for reviews for us, unless you have a very substantial online following through your blog, Facebook page, etc... And even if you do have a big following, consider copying the body of your review to Amazon, as that is the biggest marketplace in the world for books, and a review there will be most impactful. Other book-centric venues such as Goodreads and BN.com are also great, and appeal to a certain type of discerning reader. A good minimum review length to shoot for is 150 words.
- Please be HONEST. Whether you love or hate the book, or feel indifferent toward it, tell us why in a thoughtful and reflective way. The most meaningful reviews tend to be *useful,* even more than good or bad. Describe specific examples of what you did or did not like, and why.
- Other possible aspects to the review: who do you think this book would be good for? What is your background with the subject matter and why did this book come to interest you? Did it meet your expectations?
- Address concerns some readers (or fellow reviewers) might have. It is *very* useful to other

readers when one review addresses another negative review. Take a little time reading through other reviewers' comments and consider weighing in on whether the criticism leveled was valid.

That's it!

Thank you again for agreeing to this. We hope you enjoy the book, and that if you do, you'll be as motivated as we are to spread the word far and wide. We'd like nothing more than to see this book catapult up the ranks of the bestseller list and empower millions of people to self-design their own health game plan.

-Victory Belt and the whole *Solving the Paleo Equation* team

---

Rob Commentary

Eventually, when the books got shipped out, and the new deadline was put in place (reviews up between February 1 and 10), I sent out emails just about every day, checking in with our reviewers, letting them know how many reviews we had and the general sentiments expressed, and just trying to get them excited to be a part of the launch project.

One day, we had a negative review go up, and I encouraged reviewers to consider addressing those criticisms in their review and to weigh in on whether they were valid or off-base.

Each day, as they sent links and/or screenshots of their reviews, I emailed them back, thanking them, and

perhaps commenting on their review. Then I pulled their emails from the 'follow up list,' and put them on the 'completed review' list, so they would not continue to get emails from me.

And so in the end, we sent out roughly 300 review copies and got 240+ reviews out of that. A note on one thing I would do differently:

*Since we used a spreadsheet to organize the reviewer's contact information, I'd create a template document that I would send to everyone with fields already indicated so they could input their information themselves. That way, I could copy paste the reviewer's full contact details at once.

The way I did it, I had to manually enter (or copy/paste) field after field of data (name, then street address, the secondary street address, then city, then zip code, then state, then telephone number, then email address, then website, etc.) from hundreds of emails into the spreadsheet we eventually sent off to the publisher. It was an arduous process, and occasionally there'd be a transcription error, resulting in emails getting bounced back to me, and creating a second round of data input to correct the errors.

One other note: the reviewer guidelines I drafted became the basis for the standing 'review copy' offer template we have through the site. Whenever someone writes to me now asking for free review copies, I send a short note responding to them in person, and indicating that I'm copying the guidelines below. "Review them, and if interested, reply as directed. Thanks!"

Again, this creates a small hurdle to cross and gets them invested in the process more than if I simply emailed a copy without any further information. It also makes clear exactly what we expect and that this copy really is for review and not just a way to avoid paying for a copy through Amazon. That template below:

Email Template for General Catalog Books

Thanks for your interest!

As mentioned, these PDF copies are for review, and we need to make sure you're fully on board with our expectations. Here is what we need:

- You promise not to distribute your review copy anywhere else.
- You commit to a full review of at least 150 words on Amazon. Additional outlets, such as your blog, Facebook, other social media avenues, are welcome, but since we sell exclusively on Amazon, a review there will be most impactful.
- Exceptions may be made on a case by case basis to the Amazon requirement if you have a substantial following which would have more visibility than Amazon, and if copying your review there would somehow undermine your relationship with your followers. If that applies to you, please discuss this with me beforehand.
- One review copy at a time, and the review must be written within 10 days of our sending it

to you. It cannot just sit on your hard drive for weeks or months until you get around to it. If you know you won't be able to read it in that time frame, please wait until you'll have the free time and opportunity to commit to it.

- You must send me a link to your review. I will follow up with you seven days after I send you the file, and may send reminder emails as often as every day after the first week until the review is posted.
- Please be HONEST. If you love or hate the book, tell us why in a thoughtful and reflective way. The most meaningful reviews tend to be *useful,* even more than good or bad. Describe specific examples of what you did or did not like, and why.
- Other possible aspects to the review: who do you think this book would be good for? What is your background with the subject matter and why did this book come to interest you? Did it meet your expectations?
- Address concerns some readers (or fellow reviewers) might have. It is *very* useful to other readers when reviews address other negative reviews. Take a little time reading through other reviewers comments and consider weighing in on whether the criticism leveled was valid.

Still with me? If so, awesome; you're ready to

be a reviewer for us. Please reply to this email with the following subject line:
--

    I agree 100% to your review guidelines and am super, duper psyched to do it!
--

    And in the body of the email indicate:
- Your name
- What book(s) you want to review
- Avenues aside from Amazon that you aim to promote your review
- Any other questions or concerns.

    Thanks again for your interest- I look forward to your review!
    Rob

Rob Commentary

There ya have it. I hope you can glean something from this, once and future reviewperstars!

    So that's way too much information on how we filtered our list down to a lean list of people who were game to actually follow through with a review.

    We figured a few had to have been turned off by the chore of writing a review and going through this process, and/or disappointed in the book—making this ordeal feel woefully not worth the time and effort. So we decided to do one more thing of vital importance.

We sent them a gift after—a free audiobook using the Audible discount codes discussed earlier. We sent an email thanking them, offering a free audiobook of their choice (of my books, there were seven at the time), and asking them if they would like to be part of the future review team.

About 150 replied with an enthusiastic yes, and now we have a rock solid 150 people on our review team patiently awaiting whatever I write next. It's a good thing. And we'll probably repeat this process for the next book if we feel like it's really "the one" and build another 500 on top of it, going super mega and getting 500+ reviews in the first few weeks on the next release. If we feel like the expenditure is worth it, we'll definitely try that.

But Buck didn't like how the whole thing played out because we took 288 loyal fans who would have purchased a book and totally watered down the number of early purchases required to fire that book up to the top of the charts. Not only did our publishing company have to pay $3,000 for copies, it missed out on a couple thousand dollars in sales and improved ranking that could have easily led to another $1,000 in sales. In total, I figure this really cost the publishing company more like $5,000-$6,000.

Sure, I've got a nice-looking book with 250 reviews on it, only one of which is 1-star. That's great. I'm sure it will have a long shelf life because of it. But sales are pretty crappy, plus the pricing on this book was disharmonious with the price of all my other books—I'm a big fan of selling in bulk at a low price and getting more exposure, which is money in the bank for later. In essence, the sum of a few fears came true. I have a book with tons of reviews, about $3,000 was paid for these reviews, and now this book is only selling around five copies per day by my estimates (the publisher sees those stats, not me). Super. Now it will take the publisher nearly 100 days just to break even on the review copies.

That's pretty piss-poor by my standards. If that money came directly out of my pocket I would be looking of ways to improve those numbers—more reviews, less money, more sales, faster ROI. Since we did this, that's exactly what Buck has been stewing on. He's been stewin' it and stewin' it and stewin' it well. In the next chapter, Buck reveals some better strategies he has planned for self-publishing "the one" in late 2014 or early 2015.

Review Strategy 11: Gift Card Idea

Giving away review copies in exchange for a review, and leaning out your review team to only the ones who are good to go, is indeed a fine hunk of meat. But a fine hunk of meat isn't a complete stew. Buck is ready to add some mirepoix, a bouquet garni, and a sachet d'epices and other French things to his bouillabaisse. That's right ladies, Buck can cook, too!

Sorry, that was a really stewpid metaphor. I need to get souper focused and stop giving you a bunch of bullion.

Wait, did you guys catch that? This stuff just comes right off of the top of Buck's head. I think there's a future in stand-up comedy for this cat.

Here's a couple of ideas I have for releasing "the one." I hope you get what I mean when I say that. In today's modern publishing era, it takes the luck out of the game when you just publish short book after short book after short book at high volume. Almost any half-decent author, writing about subjects more popular than breeding seahorses, can churn books out these days and watch sales figures climb in a year or two to a respectable full-time income.

But when you're cranking out title after title, many of the ideas you pursue are about books that you know are destined to mediocrity and no more than a few hundred dollars per month. Most books published on Kindle fall into this "sale or two per day" category. There's no shame in that, but then there are the titles you've had kicking around in your head for years maybe, and those you know have much greater potential if you could just launch them with enough force to get seen.

I have one such title in mind, and I've had it in mind for a full decade now. Because it's so good, I haven't written it or released it. The thought of it falling flat and NOT becoming a bestseller is a tragedy in my mind that I want to avoid at all costs. Based on what I'm seeing in the self-publishing world, the rapid surge in knowledge that I've accumulated since I've been at this, and the growth trajectory of my current author fanbase, this book might finally get written in the next year. We'll see.

When I release it, you can bet that for this title I will spare no expense. That doesn't mean I don't want to be smart with those dollars though, but I'd be willing to clear out a good portion of the savings account for this big-potential piece.

I like what the review team did for the reviews. I did not like the flatness of the launch. Here are a couple of ways I thought this dilemma can be solved:

1. Give out gift cards for the review team to actually purchase the book
2. Buy the book as a gift to reviewers
3. Oh you know I'm going to use this list to waste your time
4. Rhymes with snore
5. Whack-a-doodle dandy

Both giving out gift cards for purchasing the book and gifting the book to reviewers accomplishes a few important things: no trips to the post office required, no need to gather and log a bunch of addresses, enables more international reviewers, lists the reviews as "Amazon Verified Purchases," and most importantly—*counts as a sale.*

That's right, if you give 1,000 people a $10 gift card to buy your book, and they all use it to buy your book, you get some commission back (recouping up to 70% of that expense), and your book gets propelled to the top of the Hot New Releases charts and beyond. With that comes a lot of additional paid sales coming in, recouping more of that initial expense if not all of it and then some. Plus there would be an uptick in the sales of your other books by those who liked your blockbuster.

The gift card thing is cool if you can make sure that your review team is of excellent quality through a lengthy filtering process. I mean, nothing is really stopping them from blowing it in several ways, such as: not using the card to buy your book, not using the card at all, not reading your book when they get it, not writing a review when they get it.

Some of your gift card expenditure is guaranteed to go missing.

What I like the most about the gift card approach however, is the great ease of sending out real, physical copies. All you have to do is:

1. Go to Amazon
2. Pick the email-delivered gift card
3. Click on "Select a gift"
4. Choose the book you want to send
5. Set the amount, plus a little extra if shipping is involved (hardcopy)
6. Paste all the email addresses you want in there, separated by commas
7. Fill out a little note begging them to review your book
8. Proceed through checkout
9. Rhymes with fine

10. Quack-a-noodle candy

Below is Buck pretending to send a Kindle copy of *Kill Your Blog* to the once-filtered review team of 288. I whited out the emails a little bit so you don't get any funny ideas. Themz reviewers is mine!

The big "if" remaining with this strategy is, like I said, will they actually buy the thing with the gift card you send them? Most probably will, but there will be some losses.

The other option is to lose some time and dramatically increase your purchase rate by actually gifting them a copy. As of now, you have to enter one email at a time (unless there's some trick I don't know). You could probably copy and paste about four email addresses per minute, but that's some grueling work if you're thinking of sending out free copies in the quadruple digits. I guess you can find some slave labor on Odesk for like $1 an hour though. I'd pay it, and then hang my head with guilt.

To gift a copy, just go to the regular sales page on Amazon for your book. It's says "Buy with One Click" on the right, and under that there is a "Give as a Gift" button. I think I'd have to go with the gift card method rather than gifted copy. It's just so much easier, and still would probably work just fine. I haven't tested this though. I'm not even 100% positive that these gift card purchases would qualify as sales, but as far as I know they do.

Pretty genius idea right? Turns out Buck is not the only to have had it. In fact, Amazon doesn't allow you to give a gift card for the purchase of a book as a "review copy." The only thing that qualifies as a genuine review copy is a free copy of the book. Any other form of compensation, including a gift card for the identical amount of the price of the book, is in breach of their rules. You can read a lengthy discussion about it in some reviewer forum thread here: http://amzn.to/1jc9yEo.

Amazon knows how its game works, and they consider this to be cheating in some sense. It tears Buck up inside because it's really not very fair. Mailing out physical copies sucks, it's expensive, kills a lot of innocent trees (that's right ladies, Buck has a sensitive side, too!), and many authors just aren't even bothering to make physical copies. So what the heck is a Kindle-only author to do? Just send out an unsecure PDF? Yeah right.

Well, there are still a couple of potential ways to beat the system left. I can't say definitively that they are kosher with Amazon's rules, because they really aren't. But this idea is so good, and Amazon's rules so unfair to small Kindle-only publishers going up against publishing giants sending out hundreds of review copies of every title, that I simply can't let it die easily.

If you buy gift cards, Amazon can track that, especially when you buy those gift cards on Amazon and your name happens to be the same as the author who is selling 90% of his or her books to gift card users. Fishy I tell ya. This is where Buck would seize the opportunity to crack a tasteless joke about somebody's mom. Buck loves yo' mama jokes.

So I think the only way to really conveniently give people money to buy your book, allowing your reviewers to read your book for free while everyone else has to pay—but still making sure those fans of yours getting a review copy bump up your sales rank in the paid store, is to send a mass payment to your review team through Paypal.

As an owner of multiple businesses that have an affiliate program, I am quite accustomed to sending out mass payments on Paypal. It's easy.

You click on Send Money, then Make a Mass Payment, then upload a .txt file with the names of the people and the amount paid and currency type. So, for myself (fictitious email address), I would open up Notepad on my computer and type this in:

    buckflogging@gmail.com   9.99 USD

    For my entire review team, I could have gotten a Paypal address from each and sent $9.99 to every reviewer with the anticipation that each would write a review in a timely fashion once they had used this money to purchase a copy of the book (they could actually choose the format they wanted if multiple formats were available).

    Amazon couldn't track this in any way, so while it's still slightly unjust by their policies, it's extremely unlikely that you wouldn't be able to get away with it. I wouldn't do it for all my books, but I would certainly give it some serious consideration for "the one."

    Now, this would be perfectly legal as far as I know if you didn't try to coerce these people into leaving a review. Sure, many would in exchange for a free copy, but really putting a lot of pressure on them borders violation of Amazon's review policy.

    So I don't know. You make the call on this for yourself as to whether it is "right" or "wrong." There are strong arguing points on both sides of the right/wrong debate, making this strategy fall squarely into the gray. I'm pretty certain it would work really REALLY well though in terms of making your sales rank surge while generating an exceptional number of reviews in proportion to total downloads.

Before we move on to the 12th and final strategy, let's just recap by looking at some numbers. Buck likes numbers.

Let's say hypothetically I want just flat out retarded review numbers and sales with my masterpiece book. Here's exactly what I would do based on my mental stew-du-jour, and some totally realistic numbers (I think, but who could know for sure?):

1. Tap into all of my subscriber lists that might be interested in this book by offering a free review copy via Paypal pre-imbursement. I project that a year from now that will exceed 100,000 with a broadcast open rate of 40%, meaning that 40,000 people will open an email if I send one out.

2. Send them to an info page about the review terms. Explain that they will get a small payment via Paypal equal to the price of the book, and that this money should be used to purchase the book, and that I'm expecting both a review on Amazon and a social media or website share in return.

This page will need to be very concise and direct just like Rob's email responses were about "the arrangement." This should serve as a decent quality filter.

3. Get about 5,000 people to enter their email address in an Aweber form I create.

4. Send out an autoresponse email upon entering their email address explaining once more how everything works and providing a contact email address for any questions and technical issues and stuff. Pray to Allah that they don't all decide to reply.

5. Release the book with a Kindle price of $9.99 (paperback and Audible version already made). This is the highest price that still pays out a 70% royalty share. So I get nearly $7.00 back from each copy purchased—total loss of about $3 per copy, but I expect 20% to not actually buy the book with the payment. So I lose, let's say, $3 on 4,000 copies and $10 on 1,000 copies for a total loss of $22,000.

6. Send out the 5,000 payments for ~$50,000.

7. Get 4,000 sales and 2,500 reviews in the first few weeks, almost all positive because they are my fans that already like me.

8. With improved rank and telling everybody else in my network about the book (that didn't go for the review copy thing), I sell an additional 3,000 copies averaging at least $7 per copy in royalties (Audible pays MUCH more typically with their bounty program and affiliate program). That recoups $21,000 of that $22,000 loss.
9. Use an affiliate link in my emails and get 8% extra plus commission on other Amazon items purchased within 24 hours for an additional $2,000-$3,000 already putting me in the positive.
10. Sell 1,000 total copies of my other books with an average of $5 commission each plus 500 more from the improvement in sales rank in all of my books across the board for $7,500 more.
11. Make headlines and top charts and watch that thing sell to pieces for years, with my other books selling better alongside of them and my subscriber list growing steadily all the while.
12. Keep writing until the fire department has to come chisel me out of my house because my dick is too big to drag out the door.

In reality, I'd probably make headlines for gaming the system, ruin this sweet strategy for everyone else, be branded a sleezeball for the rest of my writing career, and end up going back to the forest ranger job that I did for much of my 20's—which is a really sweet job. I don't mind it. So my worst-case scenario here isn't that bad.

Of course, with a list of 100,000 subscribers, I simply won't need to even bother with this strategy. I'll be able to achieve most of those things without buying 5,000 review copies for other people and risking both money and retribution from Mother Amazon. But I did want to demonstrate that, with the right book, the right infrastructure built up, and with the upfront capital to invest, this could work out beautifully. Perhaps I'll one day become the world's biggest Reviewperstar. I'll certainly come brag about it in an updated version of this book if I really do pull it off in 2015.

But don't blindly take my advice. It's just an idea. For heaven's sake, test it out with 20 people before you go that deep into it.

Review Strategy 12: Build a Network

After nearly a year and a half of playing the Amazon game, I can confidently say that a book's ability to perform is directly proportional to the launch force behind it. By that I mean, the stronger the debut, and the more sales in the first few days to few weeks, the more enduring that title will be. There are other factors, and lots of tricks to breathe life back into a book that is fading in the ranks, but nothing compares to that built-up launch pressure.

I was bummed in November of 2013 when I proposed to the owners of a huge blog network this idea of pooling all resources towards Amazon releases. The network had over 100 blogs working together with over 10 million unique visits per month and millions of people combined in all of their social networks. This was the perfect recipe for launching a book every week by a different author in the network.

What I proposed was that there be a regular 99-cent book promoted each Friday amongst all the participants in the network. We estimated the network to be able to trigger 10,000+ sales of each new book each week. The blog authors in the network were also going to pitch in and trade some reviews every Friday.

This was a great idea. Unfortunately, blog networks like this have so many opportunities to succeed it's hard to pick one. Even more unfortunately, all the rumors I've heard lately suggest that this network is falling apart at the seams—to be expected when the owners of the network have a formula for turning just about any blogger into a massive success. Once those bloggers become huge, it takes an awful lot of loyalty and willpower to stay in the network.

It's a real bummer, as this blog network could have effectively become what I believe to be the most powerful Kindle publishing house in the world.

It's clear that whatever you can do to form some kind of network or alliance however, the more sales and reviews you can generate. Imagine 50 authors working together carefully to cross-promote and cross-review each other's work. The potential is staggering, and I wish I was the head of such an alliance.

I will be forming a book club based on the same theme with a new project I have called 180 Radio, which will leverage podcasting to build a huge direct marketing list, in turn fueling the success of a "book club" of sorts. The book club will be just a tiny wing of 180 Radio—more like a feather, but as it grows it could become quite powerful. Same setup—a 99-cent book every Friday promoted to the list. I will call it the "Book for a Buck Friday" or "F.A.B. Friday" for short. A little gimmicky, but it should get people's attention, help little bells ring in their heads every Friday knowing that a really great book is going to be marked down to 99 cents, and create Kindle King Midas. Everything he touches turns to gold.

So, this is not necessarily a review strategy per se. In fact, co-conspiring with other authors to do review trades is a huge gray area in Amazon's Review Rules. I don't know if you should get too comfortable with the strategy. But obviously most people reading this book don't get a lot of book reviews and would like to. Presumably this lack of book reviews is due to having a relatively small audience and not being able to sell many copies or get readers to loyally review your books as a favor to you.

That's where networking comes in. It's hard to build an audience from scratch if you don't have one. You're better off networking with others in whatever way you can and piggybacking off of their pre-established audiences. I have piggybacked others as well as let many piggyback me. That's just how it works on the internet and how entities get steadily bigger and more visible.

    I won't go into too much detail on this. I've discussed this more thoroughly in *Kill Your Blog*. Suffice it to say that networking with others is much easier than you think it is. A single email can change the course of your business if you just put your big boy pants on and send it. Me n' ol Rob's publishing business, Archangel Ink, was built primarily with two emails that took me about 15 minutes to write. Of course I had some notoriety already built up, and the two of us had spent quite a bit of time building up our knowledge base to be able to provide a valuable service to others, but to reach customers we just had to send an email to two important people. By the 3rd month in business we had hauled in 30 times more money than we invested to start it.

Conclusion

I'm Buck Flogging. This has been, *Reviewperstar: 12 Tasteful Ways to get More Book Reviews.* Just as Ice Cube mistakenly felt that life was about nothing but "bitches and money," as authors we can often feel like life ain't nothing but "rank and reviews." Reviews may feel like everything, but they're not. I was plenty successful with very few reviews, and I've only been marginally more successful since finding all of these ways to open the review floodgates—some tested, some not.

I admit: I'm a slut for reviews. I just think it's fun, and my ability to get reviews now and in the years to come is going to have a tremendous impact on my status as an author—both in the eyes of the public, the eyes of big book publishers, and in the eyes of other authors and entrepreneurs.

So perhaps some time and effort to get ungodly sums of reviews really is in your best interest, even if they don't seem to have much impact in the short run.

Anyway, I think it's about time to pull the plug on this one and move onto the next project. I hope this was helpful, and that this book has a profound impact on your future career as an author. These are not the only strategies to get reviews, but they are the ones I use and hope to use in the future with great success. For more strategies, check out some of the books in the upcoming Author Resources section.

I may talk silly about all my ladies and the unprecedented largeness of my man meat, but in the end I *deeply* care about authors. I've known I was put on this earth to be an author since declaring my major as "English; Writing" at 20 years of age. Little did I know then how easy it was going to be with the modern advances in technology and book publishing.

If you have any desire burning within to be a successful writer, take advantage of these modern times. Ronnie Coleman was right when he said, "Ain't nothin' to it but to do it! Yeah buddy! Light weight! Woo! Yep! Yep!"

I mentor many authors and aspiring online entrepreneurs. Don't hesitate to reach out to me if you need my help. You can email me directly at buck@archangelink.com, and I'll gladly help you out, in many cases totally free of charge. I'd also love to hear about any of your successes and failures with some of your review strategies, or something that you think is missing from or inaccurate about this book.

Now go get those reviews! You can start by utilizing the most powerful strategy of all:

Review Strategy #8: Write Reviews

If you write a review for this book, I give you my 100% guarantee that the stars will align and conspire to get you more book reviews. Don't ask me how. Buck just knows these things! Guy's got the big G.O.D. on speed dial.

But seriously, help a brother out. You got this thing for cheap for crying out loud. It's your moral duty to write a review!

Other Recommended Author Resources

Steve Scott Books http://amzn.to/OFcAn0
Tom Corson-Knowles Books http://amzn.to/1nKpAYf
Derek Murphy's *Book Marketing is Dead*
E.T. Barton's *Get Reviews So You Can Sell More Books*

Excerpt from *How to Create an Audiobook for Audible*

Is an Audiobook Right for You?

Of course it is! What, you think we put this little book together to tell you that making an audiobook is a BAD idea? Audiobook sales are expected to grow from an estimated $200 million in 2013 to $750 million in 2016. At least, that's what I thought I read in Tom Corson Knowles's book, *Secrets of the Six-Figure Author*. I was never good at figuring out pie charts though. Yeah I read that book, shut up. I am a six-figure author so back off man! I can read whatever I want. I'll read Phil Jackson's *Sacred Hoops* if I feel like it. You should read some of Tom's books, too. Every self-published author should read them.

    I personally feel very hopeful, nay, *excited*, about the audiobook market. Smart phones come with an Audible or iTunes app already installed. Every new car has a port for your phone or iMP3Pod or whatever they call those things. It's just getting easier and easier to listen to books. So why wouldn't you? Reading is hard on the eyes anyway. And we are doing so much of it these days on computer screens that audiobooks provide a nice reprieve.

Plus, although you can read an eBook on a smartphone, it's still too small to be fun and totally kills your battery life. Listening does not. And who wants to carry around both a smartphone AND a book or eReader? With just one device and some ear buds you can still get your story on wherever you may be. And then there's driving of course. Listen while driving—yes. Read while driving—no.

Okay I'll stop. But I will say that I was fully convinced of their potential long before I saw any sales predictions on audiobooks, and the sales predictions are outrageously good.

In terms of ACTUAL sales figures, this is what I've seen recently:

- December 2013: 110 audiobooks sold
- January 2014: 155 audiobooks sold
- February 2014: 263 audiobooks sold

Growth I tellz ya!

General trends and forecasts aside, this is what I believe based on my personal experience with selling audiobooks...

You can probably count on adding about 10-20% total revenue to the sale of a book by listing it with ACX (Audiobook Creation Exchange), which lists the book on Amazon, Audible, and iTunes. So, if you are making about $1,000 per month on your book currently, publishing it in audiobook format should bump that up to $1,100-1,200 all other variables equal, although some books are a lot more conducive to becoming an audiobook than others. There are some strategies that we'll discuss that can bump that significantly higher as well.

That said, in some cases, as with one of our projects, *The Genie Within*, you may end up striking a chord with listeners and earning more with your audiobook than in paperback and Kindle sales combined, all without doing much active promotion.

Like eBooks or paperbacks published through Createspace or something similar, you will get a commission on all of the sales of your books. If the buyer entered through an affiliate link of yours, you'll get a little extra commission on top of that—same as what happens when you send someone from your website to Amazon to buy a book through an Amazon Associates affiliate link. Nothing new there. But unlike eBooks and paperbacks, there are several innovative and lucrative ways to make money off of the sale of audiobooks.

One way to make more off of the sale of your audiobook is to take advantage of Audible's great affiliate program. Audible has a 30-day free trial. If you send someone to the site to get your book (or any book for that matter) through your affiliate link, and they sign up for the free trial, you get $10. If they go on to become paying members, that jumps up to $25. Not bad. So if you have a big audience, a big subscriber list, a huge social media following, and so on—you'll likely be able to generate much more than a 10-20% bump in total revenue.

Another way you get paid is when your book is the first book downloaded by a new Audible member. When that happens, you get a $50 bounty. Yes, $50! This is another huge game-changer regarding audiobooks, and is why I think nearly everyone should go to the trouble of turning every manuscript into an audiobook.

For example, my best-selling book, *Eat for Heat*, is just a teeny tiny 20,000 words or so. I typically sell it for just $2.99 on Kindle for a royalty of just over $2. It's also available to be borrowed through the Kindle lending library, which gets me about the same $2 every time someone borrows the book.

In January of 2014 I sold about 750 Kindle downloads including borrows—about $1,500.

In comparison, I sold 40 *Eat for Heat* audiobooks in the same sales period. Not many in comparison, but this is why I think audiobooks are PFE (Pretty freakin' exciting)...

Audible prices books based on the length of the recording. *Eat for Heat* is a short one so it is priced at Audible's lowest price point, which is $6.95 as of this writing. Already I get over $3 per copy (40% commission rate if published exclusively through ACX, which is what we recommend), which is more than I get from Kindle sales. The cool thing is that out of 40 copies, a remarkable 4 qualified for the $50 bounty. That's an additional $200. Thus, I made somewhere around $350 total off of just 40 book sales. That's almost $10 per copy! Plus I got affiliate commission of over $100 that month as well.

Keep in mind that I am a nonfiction writer, and write mostly health and nutrition-related stuff. Even though fiction generally sells better, some nonfiction genres perform better than others. And in some ways nonfiction is superior to fiction because of the reduced competition and because nonfiction books tend to be shorter. This means faster production and turnaround time, and a lower final price, reducing buyer hesitation and generating more sales.

"Once upon a time there was a polyunsaturated fatty acid..."

Well, boring stuff to listen to when it's someone other than me narrating. No matter what I read, listening to my voice is like making sweet love to a schoolboy.

Oh come on! Movie reference. I would never. *Dumb and Dumber?* Jim Carrey? You guys had to have seen that one. Anyone?

So perhaps, considering my genre, these numbers are a little low. Your outcome might be better. I know one book that I narrated, *The Genie Within* by Harry Carpenter, is more of a self-helpish type of book with guided hypnosis, making it much more enticing as an audiobook than the kindle and paperback versions of it. It sells better than any of my audiobooks, yet I sell triple the amount of kindle books that Harry does. I'm pretty sure with the right strategy, Harry could make more revenue off of his audiobook than his kindle and paperback versions—if he were so inclined.

I don't know where exactly to fit this next discussion, but I wanted to point it out somewhere, and that is audiobook length and pricing as a deciding factor. This is more important to take into consideration if you are paying someone to produce your audiobook, but it's still something worthy of pointing out even for the audiobook self-producer. Like most things in the self-publishing game in the year 2014, the advantage goes to the "short, cheap, and plenty of it" strategy.

You get a $50 bounty for the sale of a book from a new Audible member. You trigger more sales of a cheap book than an expensive book, with more opportunities at a bounty. Audible prices its books based on length. I don't know exactly where the cutoffs are, but I think anything less than an hour is currently $3.95, and anything between an hour and somewhere between two and three hours is $6.95. Longer than that and price takes a big jump up to $14.95.

First, think about what a customer sees when browsing your book on Amazon. They will see a Kindle price, a paperback price (if you have one), and an audiobook price. If you're going to sell a lot of audiobooks, and you should aim for that because, like I pointed out earlier, you'll probably get more money per copy sold (and also provide the customer with a much more intimate experience—especially if you narrate it yourself)—then you want the price to be in the same ballpark.

I consider 20,000 words to be the magic number for book length these days. This gives you a book that will come out just long enough to justify paperback production (for extra sales), and the book will be just short enough to come in at $6.95 on Audible, which will probably be even cheaper than what you price your paperback. If someone has any inclination to hear the thing as an audiobook, $6.95, priced less than the paperback version even, is a steal. They're in.

It's also a small enough price that you can give a customer that little bit of extra motivation to maybe go ahead and finally become an audible member—buying yours as their first for a $50 bounty.

And, most importantly, a 2-hour audiobook isn't expensive to have done for you, nor is it such a big chore to do yourself. Hell, I turn out a fully polished, edited, mastered, 20,000-word manuscript to my clients for just $500. A longer audiobook that's priced higher and sells fewer copies, generating fewer bounties, might cost you $1,500 to pay me to record.

If that was confusing, the summary is simple. Got a 100,000-word manuscript? You probably shouldn't do an audiobook or pay someone else to do it unless you are doing it based on a royalty split with a narrator (no up-front costs) or unless that book is riding high on the bestseller lists with dozens of sales per day in Kindle and paperback.

Got a 20,000-word manuscript that's selling a few copies a day? Better turn that into an audiobook ASAP. It's a no-brainer. You can't lose unless you narrate the thing drunk while chewing gum in an empty hallway.

So I guess that's it. I just wanted to throw a little straight talk at you and let you know the things I take into consideration before deciding whether or not a book is a good candidate for audiobook production.

It might be smart to produce an audiobook. It might not be. This is not a book about getting you so psyched out of your mind, dollar signs in eyes, that you start humping Rob's leg for showing you the technical tips that are going to make your future riches possible. No need to get crazy, putting down a bunch of money to get that swimming pool put in, anticipating that big Christmas bonus from Uncle Audible.

Another movie reference and you missed it. Fine, enough with the movie references. You guys aren't even getting them. And my silliness is starting to get weird.

But I wanted to be real with you about what you can expect. You won't get a whole roast turkey, but you'll make a little gravy. It's worth it for just about every author to go ahead and just blast the audiobook out along with the Kindle version (and print-on-demand through Createspace). It's better than a 1-year subscription to the jelly of the month club for sure.

Damnit man! What's with these movie references? I can't stop! These fingers have a mind of their own when they start pressing away on the keyboard.

Financially it's an easy yes for most authors. Even indie authors. Yes you probably read that it's not worth it on a blog or two somewhere, but times are changing. Is it worth the hassle and cost though?

In the remaining chapters we have a looksee at what is involved and see if audiobook production is truly for you. Promise no more movie references.

About the Author

"Giving you the Buck-naked truth about online entrepreneurship."

Hi I'm Buck Flogging. Hell yeah that's my real name and that's totally me in the picture living large and driving the ladies wild. It's definitely not just some picture from Shutterstock.

When I'm not busy squatting 800 pounds for reps and pleasing all those ladies, I'm writing lots of books, narrating audiobooks, helping authors publish and successfully sell their work, and operating some lucrative online businesses of mine.

I originally started as a know-nothing wannabe writer that was encouraged to start this mysterious thing called a "blog." From moronic mistakes and prolonged poverty I emerged seven years later with the success that all online entrepreneurs dream of achieving.

I hope to find time to write several short books revealing as much of what I've learned as possible. I love seeing other people succeed, and I hate to see others make mistakes. For more author resources, go to www.archangelink.com. For questions or comments, send those to buck@archangelink.com

Other books by Buck:
- *Kill Your Blog: 12 Reasons Why You Should Stop $%#ing Blogging!*
- *How to Create an Audiobook for Audible*

www.ingramcontent.com/pod-product-compliance
Lightning Source LLC
Chambersburg PA
CBHW020926180526
45163CB00007B/2896